ON BEING A *Mother*

ON BEING A Mother

HEARST BOOKS

NEW YORK

Library of Congress Catalog Card Number: 89-81524
ISBN: 1-58816-028-9 (formerly 0-688-09735-9)

First U.S. Edition
5 6 7 8 9 10

Printed in Singapore

EDITED BY LINDA SUNSHINE
INTERIOR DESIGN BY BARBARA SCOTT-GOODMAN
COVER DESIGN BY ALEXANDRA MALDONADO
FRONT COVER PHOTOGRAPH (PIANO) BY JANA TAYLOR
PHOTOGRAPH (ROSES) BY GEOFFREY GROSS

PRODUCED BY SMALLWOOD & STEWART, NEW YORK CITY

INTRODUCTION

*O*ur magazine, *Victoria*, maintains a reverence for tradition and for the gentle flow of life through generations of family members. We believe that remembrance of times past brings special joy and that nothing is more sacred or closer to the heart of our readers than the joys of family. Thus, in *On Being A Mother*, we celebrate the magical, spiritual, sometimes mystical, bond that exists between mother and child.

Here we have gathered together the wisdom and philosophy about motherhood from generations of writers and married these gracious recollections to a journal format, so that our readers can chronicle their own feelings about being both a child and a mother.

Family stories are like treasured jewels, so we provide space to record Hometown Memories, Skills My Mother Taught Me, Shared Moments, Family Milestones, and Traditions. Such personal recollections are enhanced by a wealth of quotations from the pages of *Victoria* and from beloved writers such as Colette, Eudora Welty, Simone de Beauvoir, Charles Dickens, Dylan Thomas, Gerald Durrell, John Mortimer, Romain Gary, Emily Dickinson, and many, many others.

It is our hope that, through the pages of this volume, women will explore their deepest feelings about being a mother and, at the same time, create a true family heirloom to pass down to future generations.

The Editors, Victoria

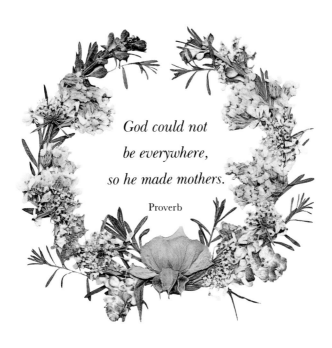

*God could not
be everywhere,
so he made mothers.*

Proverb

$\mathscr{R}$omance fails us
and so do friendships
but the relationship of
Mother and Child
remains indelible and indestructible—
the strongest bond upon this earth.

Theodor Reik

MOTHER'S GIFTS

FROM THE HEART

I should like to pay special tribute to my mother, to whom this book is dedicated. Like a gentle, enthusiastic, and understanding Noah, she has steered her vessel full of strange progeny through the stormy seas of life with great skill, always faced with the possibility of mutiny, always surrounded by the dangerous shoals of overdraft and extravagance, never being sure that her navigation would be approved by the crew, but certain that she would be blamed for anything that went wrong. That she survived the voyage is a miracle, but survive it she did, and, moreover, with her reason more or less intact. As my brother Larry rightly points out, we can be proud of the way we have brought her up; she is a credit to us.

Gerald Durrell
My Family and Other Animals

From the Heart

THE PRELUDE
OR GROWTH OF A POET'S MIND

. . . blest the Babe,

Nursed in His Mother's arms, who sinks to sleep

Rocked on his Mother's breast; who with his soul

Drinks in the feelings of his Mother's eye!

For him, in one dear Presence, there exists

A Virtue, which irradiates and exalts

Objects through widest intercourse of sense

No outcast he, bewildered and depressed:

Along his infant veins are interfused

The gravitation and filial bond

Of nature that connect him with the world.

William Wordsworth

✿

*M*y sole consolation when I went upstairs for the night was that Mamma would come in and kiss me after I was in bed. But this good-night lasted for so short a time: she went down again so soon that the moment in which I heard her climb the stairs, and then caught the sound of her garden dress of blue muslin, from which hung little tassels of plaited straw, rustling along the double-doored corridor, was for me a moment of the keenest sorrow. So much did I love that good night that I reached the stage of hoping that it would come as late as possible, so as to prolong the time of respite during which Mamma would not yet have appeared.

Marcel Proust
Swann's Way

Mother wore her hair in a pompadour, and I can still see
her, in an evening dress and coat, coming down the stairs to
go out with my father. She was always gentle and quiet.
She had a fantastic memory, was well-read, and knew the
"Rubyaiyat" by heart. She believed in discipline and
afternoon naps. The neighborhood children didn't have to
take naps, and we'd lean out the window talking to them
until we were found out, and then we were supposed to go
back to bed and rest.

Adele Kanaley Miller Christensen
My Mother Before Me

Victoria

MEMOIRS OF A DUTIFUL DAUGHTER

I did not look upon my mother as a saint, because I knew her too well and because she lost her temper far too easily; but her example seemed to me all the more unassailable because of that: I, too, was able to, and therefore ought to, emulate her in piety and virtue. The warmth of her affection made up for her unpredictable temper. If she had been more impeccable in her conduct, she would have been more remote, and would not have had such a profound effect upon me.

Her hold over me stemmed indeed a great deal from the very intimacy of our relationship. My father treated me like a fully developed person; my mother watched over me as a mother watches over a child; and a child I still was. She was more indulgent toward me than he: she found it quite natural that I should be a silly little girl, whereas my stupidity only exasperated my father; she was amused by my childish sayings and scribblings; he found them quite unfunny. I wanted to be taken notice of; but fundamentally I needed to be accepted for what I was, with all the deficiencies of my age; my mother's tenderness assured me that this wish was a justifiable one.

Simone de Beauvoir

A CHANGEABLE MOTHER

inerva," Birdeen had asked, while she combed my hair, "are you still taking on over this apron?"

Birdeen had made me long-sleeved, high-necked aprons to wear to school so that my dresses would stay clean and not wear out. No one else wore aprons to school. "They'll laugh at me," I had told my mother.

"They will not," Birdeen had replied. "You've got too much spunk for that. You'll stare them down."

By Friday I had done so. So it wasn't my apron that was making me unhappy.

"I just got out of bed blue," I had told my mother. "I don't know why."

Mama understood that. I felt the

brush strokes soften. Named difficulties, Birdeen made light of. Step on a rusty nail, sneeze your head off, go to school togged out like a scarecrow: Birdeen expected her children to overcome little troubles like those. But nameless sorrow, a heavy heart, or a longing for something, you didn't know what; if that was your trouble, Birdeen bestirred herself.

"Ginerva," she had said, beginning to brush again with her accustomed vigor, "listen while I recite my piece for tomorrow night. You know it as well as I do. Prompt me if I forget. Tell me if I'm too loud or too fast. Or don't have enough expression."

I was completely taken in. I had to put away my nameless sorrow for Mama's sake. Birdeen was entered in the elocution contest sponsored by the Valencia branch of the Women's Christian Temperance Union. As a girl back East, Birdeen had been an elocution star. The house was filled with prizes she had won: hand-blown paperweights, hand-painted hair receivers, *The Dolly Dialogues* in white leather, title in gold leaf. She was a born reciter, perhaps even an actress. There was a marked resemblance between Birdeen and Sarah Bernhardt; and Birdeen must have known it, for she frizzed her hair in an exact copy of Bernhardt's. Since her marriage, Birdeen hadn't had time or, in California, the opportunity for elocution. Now, with a contest to be held in the church to forward the cause of temperance, it was her duty to perform.

That morning, listening to Mama recite "Kentucky Belle," I had forgotten my blues . . . .

Birdeen had big gray-green eyes and long, though not thick, eyelashes. Her eyes were set in shallow sockets so that they lifted her eyelids when she closed them. Her hair was chestnut with reddish threads. Some people, seeing her in the sunlight, called her a redhead. No one ever called her a redhead more than once. Redheads, in her opinion, were coarse, hot-tempered, and unreliable, none of which Birdeen had any intention of being. She had a lot of hair but it was straight as a stick, slippery as the wind, and not all of her work with a curling iron was able to change this. Her nose was large and a little crooked, and so was her mouth. Her teeth were almost, but not quite, buck. This gave her the look of having something on the tip of her tongue to say—and this, most of the time, was actually the case.

I did not consider Mama good-looking. Reno was the looker in the family. Everyone was agreed on this. Nevertheless, I spent more time looking at my mother than at my father. There was no point in detailing Reno's face. Maybe he was as handsome as a Greek god; but like all the Greek gods I had seen in pictures, his face did not alter from minute to minute. Birdeen's did, especially when she was reciting. When my mother recited, she was "carried away," she "forgot herself." Sometimes this was frightening. Having a changeable mother was interesting, but having a mother who disappeared before your eyes was the next thing to watching her abandon you—or die.

Jessamyn West
The State of Lonesome

HER GIFTS TO ME

I know my mother only by her influence— far too extensive to go into here. She taught me a love for so many things—to mention a few: Gershwin, Sinatra, and "Lucy Ricardo;" foreign languages, the study of "Man," which later expanded into a passion for feminism; music, which she played on piano, especially classical and jazz; comedy and drama (she loved Sid Caesar, Ernie Kovacs, George Sanders, Alec Guiness, Cary Grant, Bette Davis, Diana Rigg); dance—ballet, modern, ballroom (she used to madly fox trot around the living room, teasing my dad about being a lousy dancer); modern art and architecture; the tantalizing mix of skepticism and romance, science and mysticism; the beauties of forces of Nature and the greater Cosmos.

Julie Kettle Gundlach
My Mother Before Me

My Mother's Gifts to Me

_____

_____

_____

_____

_____

_____

_____

_____

_____

_____

_____

A mother's hardest to forgive.
*   Life is the fruit she longs to hand you,*
Ripe on a plate. And while you live
Relentlessly she understands you.

Phyllis McGinley
The Adversary

Tell me, Praise, and tell me, Love,
What you both are thinking of?
'O, we think,' said Love, said Praise,
'Now of children and their ways.'

William Brighty Rands
Praise and Love

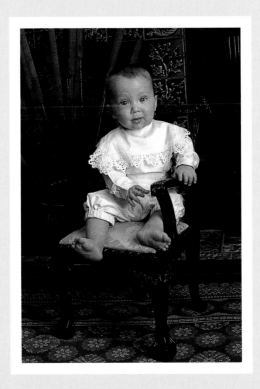

CHILDREN

M aternity! ecstatic sound!

so twined round our heart,

that it must cease to throb ere we forget it,

it is our first love,

it is part of our religion.

The Ladies Museum
1825

I desire to be a mother—if only to give food to the craving activity of my soul . . . . Maternity is an enterprise in which I have opened an enormous stake . . . . Motherhood will develop my energy, enlarge my heart, and compensate me for all things by infinite joys!

Honoré de Balzac
Memoirs of Two Young Married Women, 1894

Thoughts on Becoming a Mother

_____

_____

_____

_____

_____

_____

_____

_____

_____

_____

*Everybody knows that a good mother gives her children a
feeling of trust and stability. She is the one they can count on
for the things that matter most of all. She is their food and
their bed and their extra blanket when it grows cold in the
night; she is their warmth and health and their shelter; she is
the one they want to be near when they cry. She is the only
person in the whole world or in a whole lifetime who can be
these things to her children. There is no substitute for her.
Somehow even her clothes feel different to her children's hands
from anybody else's clothes. Only to touch her skirt or her
sleeve makes a troubled child feel better.*

Katharine Butler Hathaway
The Journals and Letters of the Little Locksmith

Victoria

My Children's Birthdays and Namesakes

". . . the daughter is for the mother at once
her double and another person."

Simone de Beauvoir
The Second Sex

Sons are the anchors of a mother's life.

Sophocles
Phaedra

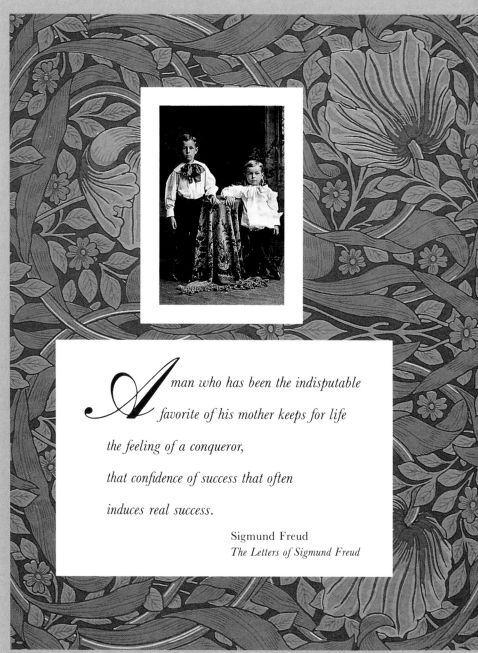

A man who has been the indisputable favorite of his mother keeps for life the feeling of a conqueror, that confidence of success that often induces real success.

Sigmund Freud
The Letters of Sigmund Freud

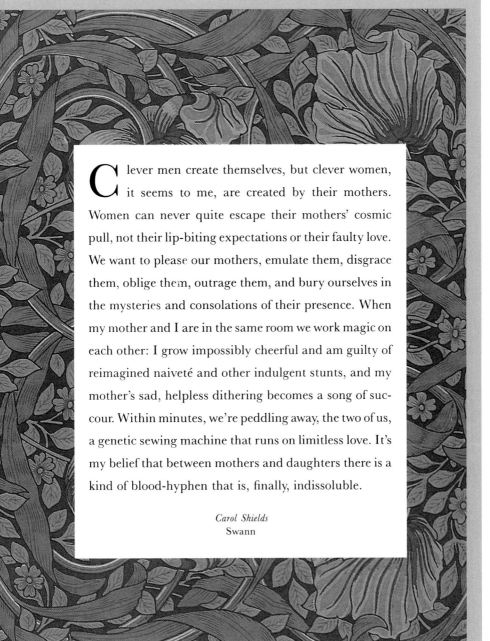

C lever men create themselves, but clever women, it seems to me, are created by their mothers. Women can never quite escape their mothers' cosmic pull, not their lip-biting expectations or their faulty love. We want to please our mothers, emulate them, disgrace them, oblige them, outrage them, and bury ourselves in the mysteries and consolations of their presence. When my mother and I are in the same room we work magic on each other: I grow impossibly cheerful and am guilty of reimagined naiveté and other indulgent stunts, and my mother's sad, helpless dithering becomes a song of succour. Within minutes, we're peddling away, the two of us, a genetic sewing machine that runs on limitless love. It's my belief that between mothers and daughters there is a kind of blood-hyphen that is, finally, indissoluble.

Carol Shields
Swann

O utside, in the slanting beams of the sun, Jenny Blair strapped on her roller-skates and started dangerously over the sunken bricks of the pavement. Her mother had told her to keep on the sunny side of the street and not to skate beyond the corner, where the bricks were uneven and loose at the edges; but experience had shown her that it was safe to interpret broadly her mother's directions.

Ellen Glasgow
The Sheltered Life

*M*others for miles around worried about Zuckerman's
swing. They feared some child would fall off. But no
child ever did. Children almost always hang onto things
tighter than their parents think they will.

E. B. White
Charlotte's Web

*H*ow she loved Joanna, through and through. What agonies she had suffered over the child, over her looks, her clumsiness, her fearful obstinacy, her fits of temper, her secrecy, her nonsense, her lack of even decent pride, her vulnerability. No one could suffer like Joanna for her own follies. And no one was more helpless than her mother to save her from the least of them.

Joyce Cary
The Captive and the Free

TO MY FOUR-YEAR-OLD DAUGHTER

I lost my temper twice today,
Once when you ordered me around like a maid,
And once when you picked all the unripe plums
from our tree.
You said I yelled so much it made you sleepy,
Popped in your thumb and drifted away.
Then, imagining you sad, I felt guilty.
You, my firstborn child, my beautiful girl.
Remember when your ear hurt and we rocked all night.
How many hours, awake, I stared in your face
Seeing prongs that reach
Deep in your childhood, deep in mine.

Gail Todd
Family Way

DOMESTIC AFFAIRS

It was a few hours later that the memory came to me of something eerily similar that my own mother had done, one spring twenty years before. I had just got a new Skipper doll—to cheer me up, because my father had been in the hospital. I'd taken the doll outside and lost her shoe. My mother had spent an hour on her hands and knees, helping me search for that shoe in the thick grass. My mother—who, I always believed, could do anything—found it.

I always tell that story with affection, but I have always made fun of my mother a little for that too. What a lot of fuss to make over something so small, I have thought to myself.

Only the fuss was about something besides a doll's shoe, of course. It was about loss and pain. Small pain, minor loss, in the scale of things. The kind of pain a mother can still control, can still prevent, maybe. Knowing, all the while, how many other sorrows there will be that she can't do anything about: Little girls who don't come to her party. Children on the playground who make fun of her overalls. Boys who ask someone else to the dance instead. Colleges she won't get into. A lover who leaves.

Joyce Maynard

Earliest Recollections

EVERYTHING GROWS IN MY MOTHER'S GARDEN

verything grows in
my mother's garden:
Camellias, delicate pinks
and whites, splendid scarlets,
Graceful lilies, regal iris,
cheerful ranunculus.

Good things to eat grow in
my mother's garden.
Tomatoes as sweet as fruit,
peppers red and green,
Carrots, sugar peas, baby lettuce.

'Coleslaw grows in my Nena's garden.'
That's what my son brags to his friends.
A city child, he thinks magic transforms
garden treats into his favorite dish.

It is magic, I tell him,
Nena's magic. Her grace
with all things green and
growing.
There must be special secrets
in my mother's garden.

All of us, family and friends,
We marvel at my mother's garden,
She must know secrets,
we think.

And, she does—
Secrets of generosity,
kindness, compassion,
Of life lived honestly,
imaginatively, well.

Still trim in gardening clothes,
She brushes dirt and leaves
from her hands
And comes to greet us.

There's much I wish I learned
from my mother:
French seams,
Southern chicken, patience,
painting, some medicine.
For these things I have no aptitude.

But now, a mother myself, I
crave a secret or two.
I want a garden, as she does
With grace and love
and skill.

We ordered bulbs together
this summer. She claims to
envy me my tulips. And I?
I want only this,
My son to say one day:

Everything grows in my
mother's garden.

Linda Peterson

*B*efore becoming a mother I had a hundred theories on how to bring up children. Now I have seven children and only one theory: love them, especially when they least deserve to be loved.

Kate Samperi

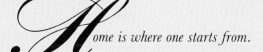
*H*ome is where one starts from.

T. S. Eliot
East Coker

H O M E

Mid pleasures and palaces though we may roam,
Be it ever so humble, there's no place like home.

John Howard Payne
"Home Sweet Home"
from the opera
Clari, The Maid of Milan

The House Where I Was Born

_____

_____

_____

_____

_____

_____

A man travels the world over in search of what he needs
and returns home to find it.

George Moore
The Brook Kerith

My mother and I walk through the rooms of her house . . . My mother and I find this a beautiful house. The rooms are large and empty, opening on to each other, waiting for people and things to fill them up. Our white muslin skirts billow up around our ankles, our hair hangs straight down our backs as our arms hang straight at our sides. I fit perfectly in the crook of my mother's arm, on the curve of her back, in the hollow of her stomach. We eat from the same bowl, drink from the same cup; when we sleep, our heads rest on the same pillow. As we walk through the rooms, we merge and separate, merge and separate; soon we shall enter the final stage of our evolution.

Jamaica Kincaid
"My Mother"

PROMISE AT DAWN

Often, when my mother returned exhausted and frozen from her rounds, the owner of the building would be waiting for her on the stairs and shout at her, threatening to throw us into the street if the rent wasn't paid within twenty-four hours. It was always paid, though how I shall never know. All I can say is that the rent was always paid, the stove lit, tea, bread,

butter and eggs were put before me, and my mother would kiss me, her eyes aglow with that bright flame of pride and triumph which I so well remember. We were then truly at the very bottom—I won't say at the bottom of the "abyss" because I have since learned that the abyss is bottomless and that all records of falling and sinking can be broken there without ever exhausting the possibilities of that interesting institution. Often, when she had come back from her expeditions through the snow-blanketed town, and had stacked her hatboxes in a corner, my mother would sit down, light a cigarette, cross her legs and look at me with a knowing smile.

"What is it, Mother?"

"Nothing. Give me a kiss."

I would kiss her. She held me in her arms, her eyes fixed over my shoulder on some mysterious, bright point in our future, visible only to her in the magical land where all the beauty lies.

"You are going to be a French ambassador," she would say, or rather state, with absolute conviction; I had not the slightest idea what the word meant, but that did not in the least keep me from agreeing with her. I was only eight, but I had already made up my mind: whatever my mother wanted I would accomplish for her—there was absolutely nothing that I would let stand in the way.

"You are going to be a French ambassador."

"Good," I would say with a nonchalant air.

Aniela, sitting close to the stove, gave me a respectful look, while my mother wiped her tears of happiness and hugged me tight.

"You will have a motor car."

She had been walking the streets all day, with the temperature well below freezing.

"All it will take is a little patience."

Romain Gary

"Y ou getting to be," she said, putting her hand beneath his chin and holding his face away from her, "a right big boy. You going to be a mighty fine man, you know that? Your mamma's counting on you."

And he knew again that she was not saying everything she meant; in a kind of secret language she was telling him something that he must remember and understand tomorrow. He watched her face, his heart swollen with love for her and with an anguish, not yet his own, that he did not understand and that frightened him. "Yes, Ma," he said, hoping that she would realize, despite his stammering tongue, the depth of his passion to please her.

James Baldwin
Go Tell It On The Mountain

A DOG'S TALE

My father was a St. Bernard, my mother was a collie, but I am a Presbyterian. This is what my mother told me; I do not know these nice distinctions myself. To me they are only fine large words meaning nothing. My mother had a fondness for such; she liked to say them, and see other dogs look surprised and envious, as if wondering how she got so much education. But, indeed, it was not real education; it was only show: she got the words by listening in the dining-room and drawing-room when there was company, and by going with the children to Sunday-school and listening there; and whenever she heard a large word she said it over to herself many times, and so was able to keep it until there was a dogmatic gathering in the neighborhood, then she would get it off, and surprise and distress them all, from pocket-pup to mastiff, which rewarded her for all her trouble. If there was a stranger he was nearly sure to be suspicious, and when he got his breath again he would ask her what it meant. And she always told him. He was never expecting this, but thought he would catch her; so when she told him, he was the one that looked ashamed, whereas he had thought it was going to be she. The others were always waiting for this, and glad of it and proud of her, for they knew what was going to happen, because they had had experience. When she told the meaning of a big word they were all so taken up with admiration that it never occurred to any dog to doubt if it was the right one; and that was natural, because, for one thing, she answered up so promptly that it seemed like a dictionary speaking, and for another thing, where could they find out whether it was right or not? for she was the only cultivated dog there was. By and by, when I was older, she brought home the word Unintellectual, one time, and worked it pretty hard all the week at different gatherings, making much unhappiness and despondency; and it was at this time that I noticed that during that week she was asked for the meaning at eight different assemblages, and flashed out a fresh definition every time, which showed me that she had more presence of mind than culture, though I said nothing, of course. She had one word which she always kept on hand, and ready, like a life-preserver, a kind of emergency word to strap on when she was likely to get washed overboard in a sudden way—that was the word Synonymous. When she happened to fetch out a long word which had had its day weeks before and its prepared meanings gone to her dump-pile, if there was a stranger there of course it knocked him groggy for a couple of minutes, then he would come to, and by that time she would be away down the wind on another tack, and not expecting anything; so when he'd hail and ask her to cash in, I (the only dog

on the inside of her game) could see her canvas flicker a moment—but only just a moment—then it would belly out taut and full, and she would say, as calm as a summer's day, "It's synonymous with supererogation," or some godless long reptile of a word like that, and go placidly about and skim away on the next tack, perfectly comfortable, you know, and leave that stranger looking profane and embarrassed, and the initiated slatting the floor with their tails in unison and their faces transfigured with a holy joy.

And it was the same with phrases. She would drag home a whole phrase, if it had a grand sound, and play it six nights and two matinées, and explain it a new way every time—which she had to, for all she cared for was the phrase; she wasn't interested in what it meant, and knew those dogs hadn't wit enough to catch her, anyway. Yes, she was a daisy! She got so she wasn't afraid of anything, she had such confidence in the ignorance of those creatures. She even brought anecdotes that she had heard the family and the dinner-guests laugh and shout over; and as a rule she got the nub of one chestnut hitched onto another chestnut, where, of course, it didn't fit and hadn't any point; and when she delivered the nub she fell over and rolled on the floor and laughed and barked in the most insane way, while I could see that she was wondering to herself why it didn't seem as funny as it did when she first heard it. But no harm was done; the others rolled and barked too, privately ashamed of themselves for not seeing the point, and never suspecting that the fault was not with them and there wasn't any to see.

You can see by these things that she was of a rather vain and frivolous character; still, she had virtues, and enough to make up, I think. She had a kind heart and gentle ways, and never harbored resentments for injuries done her, but put them easily out of her mind and forgot them; and she taught her children her kindly way, and from her we learned also to be brave and prompt in time of danger, and not to run away, but face the peril that threatened friend or stranger, and help him the best we could without stopping to think what the cost might be to us. And she taught us not by words only, but by example, and that is the best way and the surest and the most lasting. Why, the brave things she did, the splendid things! she was just a soldier; and so modest about it—well, you couldn't help admiring her, and you couldn't help imitating her; not even a King Charles spaniel could remain entirely despicable in her society. So, as you see, there was more to her than her education.

When I was well grown, at last, I was sold and taken away, and I never saw her again. She was broken-hearted, and so was I, and we cried; but she comforted me as well as she could, and said we were sent into this world for a wise and good purpose, and must do our duties without repining, take our life as we might find it, live it for the best good of others, and never mind about the results; they were not our affair. She said men who did like this would have a noble and beautiful reward by and by in another world, and although we animals would not go there, to do well and right without reward would give to our brief lives a worthiness and dignity which in itself would be a reward. She had gathered these things from time to time when she had gone to the Sunday-school with the children, and had laid them up in her memory more carefully than she had done with those other words and phrases; and she had studied them deeply, for her good and ours. One may see by this that she had a wise and thoughtful head, for all there was so much lightness and vanity in it.

So we said our farewells, and looked our last upon each other through our tears; and the last thing she said— keeping it for the last to make me remember it the better, I think—was, "In memory of me, when there is a time of danger to another do not think of yourself, think of your mother, and do as she would do."

Do you think I could forget that? No.

Mark Twain
The Complete Short Stories
of Mark Twain

Family Pets

_____

_____

_____

_____

_____

_____

_____

_____

_____

_____

_____

MOTHER'S REMEDY

"**A**nd here is my sweet little An-namaria," she added, tenderly caressing a little girl of three years old, who had not made a noise for the last two minutes. "And she is always so gentle and quiet—never was there such a quiet little thing!"

But unfortunately, in bestowing these embraces, a pin in her ladyship's head-dress slightly scratching the child's neck, produced from this pattern of gentleness such violent screams as could hardly be outdone by any creature professedly noisy. The mother's consternation was excessive; but it could not surpass the alarm of the Miss Steeles, and every-thing was done by all three, in so critical an emergency, which affection could suggest as likely to assuage the agonies of the littler sufferer. She was seated in her mother's lap, covered with kisses, her wound bathed in lavender-water by one of the Misses Steeles, who was on her knees to attend her, and her mouth stuffed with sugar-plums by the other. With such a reward for her tears, the child was too wise to cease crying. She still screamed and sobbed lustily, kicked her two brothers for offering to touch her, and all their united soothings were ineffectual till Lady Middleton luckily remembered that in a scene of similar distress last week, some apricot mar-malade had been successfully applied for a bruised temple, the same remedy was eagerly proposed for this unfortu-nate scratch, and a slight intermission of screams in the young lady on hearing it, gave them reason to hope that it would not be rejected. She was carried out of the room therefore in her mother's arms, in quest of the medicine . . .

Jane Austen
Sense and Sensibility

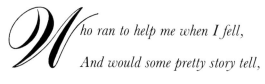

Who ran to help me when I fell,

And would some pretty story tell,

Or kiss the place to make it well?

My mother.

Ann Taylor
"My Mother"

THE JOYS OF BEING SICK IN BED

Even illness has its own special menu at our house.

It would begin when my mother declared me officially sick—sick enough to stay home from school and, therefore, sick enough to stay in bed. Immediately the day took on a holiday air and I resigned myself to bedded-down luxury, helpless in the face of nature.

The illnesses I remember most were the head colds and grippes of winter, and my progress in recovering could be measured by the food my mother served, for she always had strong ideas on exactly what one should eat when. Miraculously, her instinct seemed infal- lible, and when I did not know what I wanted, she did.

Meals always appeared on pretty trays, set with colorful mats, the best china and silver, and, when possible, a flower. . . .

All my childhood illnesses seemed to have a prescribed number of days in bed. . . . By the time I was able to have a full-scale meat and potatoes dinner, I was also able to be out of bed and dressed, and I knew the period of luxury had ended, and I felt cured, and very well cared for and loved.

Mimi Sheraton
From My Mother's Kitchen

And the best bread
was of my mother's own making—
the best in all the land!

Sir Henry James
Old Memories

Favorite Family Recipes

_____

_____

_____

_____

_____

_____

_____

_____

_____

A GRANDMOTHER'S RITUAL

When I was a girl, on chill late-November afternoons I would see the postman staggering up the drive with a brown-paper-wrapped parcel. In a flash I would run down to meet him—I knew that inside the package was an enormous tin box trimmed with Victorian gold-paper curlicues and filled with heavenly cookies baked by a lifelong friend of my mother's. This woman had a passion for uncommon flavors, and as she lived far away, she made the cookies as a way of being close to us at holiday time.

Each year there were different cookies, all traditional, all special, and carefully fitted between layers of cardboard. One year there might be springerles, which are silvery anise-flavored cookies shaped like tiles and on which a design has been pressed by a hand-carved rolling pin. Another year might bring the pure and classical shortbread the Scots call petticoat tails, fluted rounds shaped like the hooped petticoats of Scottish court ladies. Or perhaps the box would be filled with Linzer slices, rich hazelnut pastry with hints of cocoa, lemon, cinnamon, and clove, latticed over raspberry preserves. Or cinnamon stars, a very old European cookie made in America since Colonial times. Cut with a small six-pointed star, these cookies are poufs of nutted meringue flavored with cinnamon, frosted with meringue, and carefully baked so the star stays white.

Our friend always sent the tin just after the Thanksgiving holiday so that the cookies could ripen. And each year

my mother had to find a new hiding place so the cookies would ripen! It was a ritual that the box be produced when we began to decorate for the holidays. And a handful of the marvelous cookies would be our treat at the end of each decorating turn.

My mother was a joyous celebrant, and it always took many long hours to dress the house for Christmas. When my mother and I, exhausted but pleased, collapsed into whatever chairs were not heaped with decorations, my father, in his role as The Great Appreciator, would join us and warm himself by the fire's dying embers and, of course, sample some of those tasty cookies.

After Christmas, when the beautiful tin held only crumbs, my mother would shake it out for the blue jays, tuck in a fruitcake ("Never return a vessel empty," she told me), and mail it back. The following year it was returned to us, filled again with a new assortment of cookies.

Those cookies made a lasting impression. Each morsel was rich not only in evocative flavor and beauty, but also in our friend's love. From her hands and hearth and heart to ours. With every mouthful, I felt cherished.

The time came when I wanted to bake the incomparable cookies myself. Our friend generously sent me her recipe for petticoat tails. Soon I was baking all types of cookies with a passion. Off to friends both near and far went parcels of Linzer slices and cinnamon stars and petticoat tails.

A generation in our family has come and gone too quickly. Our children, who grew up loving these cookies, have scattered and now have children of their own. These days, I have several big tin boxes of my own to send. Just after Thanksgiving, I pull them down from their shelf and fill them with magical Christmas cookies and my love.

Sylvia Thompson

A COOKING HOUSE

My mother was small and round, with beautiful jade-green eyes, a regally elongated nose, a firm mouth and chin. She was funny when she meant to be and often when she didn't. Popular and sociable, she loved to entertain. Apart from family occasions, she gave fund-raising luncheons, dinner parties, and late-night suppers, and I loved the preparation that included not only the special elegant foods, but the setting out of table appointments as well. . . .

Ours was in every way a cooking house. Whenever we wanted to find my mother, we first looked in the kitchen. Sometimes I did my homework on the big kitchen table, and as I worked and we talked, I absorbed the basics of cooking simply by observing, however subliminally, the general goings-on. As a result, I cannot remember a time when I did not know how to cook.

Mimi Sheraton
From My Mother's Kitchen

It is odd how all men develop the notion, as they grow older, that their mothers were wonderful cooks. I have yet to meet a man who will admit that his mother was a kitchen assassin, and nearly poisoned him.

Robertson Davies
The Table Talk of Samuel Marchbanks

Recipes from My Mother's Kitchen

*It is good to be alone in a garden
at dawn or dark so that all its shy presences
may haunt you and possess you in a reverie
of suspended thought.*

James Douglas
Down Shoe Lane

*N*ot long ago, a little boy of my close acquaintance, only eighteen months old, and of a rare zest and energy, was given a saffron-colored crocus by his mother. His delight was boundless. He took it carefully in his small fist and so fell asleep with it unharmed. When she looked in on him later in the evening, it had come into bloom.

Walter de la Mare
Love

M O T H E R ' S   D A Y

Behind Mother were the French doors that open onto what is called in Southern California "an outdoor living room"—really, a greenhouse made of lathes and covered, in this case, with an enormous wisteria vine. Through the doors I could see Alban stretched full length in the canopied glider, reading the *Post* . . . The air was heavy with the scent of the wisteria vine, which was in full bloom, and of the Valencia groves, which were in bloom, too, and added their fragrance to that of the wisteria. Strong though they were, heavy and musky and sweet, these scents did not enter Mother's thickly curtained, heavily carpeted room very freely. Mother wants to be indoors or out; she likes definite boundaries. . . .

Outside the creak of the glider had ceased.

"Why don't you take Alban a glass of lemonade?" Mother asked.

Mother is always alert to find ways I can please Alban. She was happy when Alban came courting. I think she was afraid I might be an old maid. I know she didn't think me very attractive as a girl. It hurt me then, but I understand it better now. She didn't like her own looks and I was her spit and image. If you don't like your own looks, it is irritating, I suppose, to see them popping out at you on unexpected occasions and from unexpected angles. Mirrors you can avoid, but a young daughter has to be with you at least part of the time. Who made Mother think she was unattractive? Not my father. Father and Mother never came home from anyplace, church, or party, that he didn't say, "Ethel, you were far and away the best-looking woman there." He would stand off, cocking his head as if to truly assess her, then repeat after this deliberate scanning, "Far and away. Far and away."

And it was the truth. He wasn't simply reassuring her, or flattering her. What she thinks now of the face we have in common I don't know. Someday I'm going to ask her. I looked at her against the light of the French windows: head, with its puff of gunmetal hair, not gray but ash blond darkened, held to one side as she listened for the sound of the glider to announce that Alban was once more at ease. Her pink lips were full and pleasant over her teeth, which have a slight outward slant; her eyes, big and shining, are sea blue and flecked as that blue always is with green. And all of her, from the gunmetal hair to the finger mangled in a corn chopper when she was a girl, alive and shining in spite of her sixty years. . . .

Anyway, that's my face, too, minus twenty-five years. And while I admit, as I read recently, that no woman with a

long upper lip can be *pretty*, still we're not as plain as Mother thinks. But the habit, early formed, of compensating to Alban for my lack of beauty still persists. I got the pitcher of lemonade from the refrigerator, poured a glass, and took it to him.

The lathe house under its canopy of blossoming wisteria was a big purple cave. So beautiful! I felt loving toward the whole human race simply to think that it was capable of developing a vine like the wisteria and of training it over a support like a lathe house so that for a week or two in spring there would exist a room lined with amethysts and scented like honey. The light was lavender colored. Bees seemed to be hanging in the air. And over all the dry, homesick rustle of palms along the driveway.

"It's like being in a big, sweet purple cave," I told Alban.

He was deep in his story and didn't hear me. He drained the glass, put it down, and said, "Your mother's never happy unless she's feeding someone, is she?"

"I wouldn't say never."

He shook the seeds in the bottom of the glass. "Got any more?"

"Lots more," I said, and fetched the pitcher.

"I knew he'd like it," my mother told me as I went out with it.

Jessamyn West

*T*o me the smell of Roses is invariably calming. Over and over again I have experienced the quieting influence of Rose scent upon a disturbed state of mind, feeling the troubled condition smoothing out before I realized that Roses were in the room, or near at hand.

Louise Beebe Wilder
Pleasures of the Nose

Favorite Flowers

_____

_____

_____

_____

_____

_____

_____

T here is a great abundance of safe, healthful, and delightful recreations, which all parents may secure for their children. . .   One of the most useful and important, is the cultivation of flowers and fruits. This, especially for the daughters of a family, is greatly promotive of health and amusement . . .   It would be a most desirable improvement, if all schools for young women could be furnished with suitable grounds and instruments for the cultivation of fruits and flowers, and every inducement offered to engage the pupils in this pursuit.

Catharine Beecher and Harriet Beecher Stowe
Gardening and the Education of Women

The first strawberry shrub that I ever saw was given to me when a small child by a red-cheeked boy just as I went into church with my grandmother. I slipped it into the palm of my hand under my glove, and throughout the service I kept my nose closely to the opening of the glove, smelling the flower. I was reproved again and again, but I continually reverted to my new and exquisite diversion; for, in those days, the time spent in church seemed longer than the rest of the whole week. Even now, each spring, when the first of these strange little flowers gives its scent to the air, I am for an instant transplanted, as it were, back to that stiff church pew, aching to be out in the open, and smelling the strawberry shrub in my glove.

Alice Lounsberry
Gardens of Sweet Scent

A FAMILY HOME

My son journeyed into this house that had been his great-grandparents' in a baby basket. As we lunched in the breakfast room, the midday sun filtering through the windows glistening clean, he slept peacefully beside me. It did not seem warm at all that day—thick walls and shade trees outside were effective air coolers.

This will be the last summer we shall return to this grand old house. It is now too big for its residents to manage, and no one in the family is left to carry on the traditions that have been born and bred here.

The sun porch is now jammed with cardboard boxes—all neatly packed, all destined for different parts of the country where relatives will receive bequests so carefully considered. Aunt Mary is seeing to that. For years now she has been the curator of this family home—and never has there been a better one. Even on this day the windows sparkle like diamonds and, flung open to catch the breeze, they remind me of calm, cool days spent on that porch chatting, drinking iced tea, and eating frosted creams, one of the family's cherished recipes. No one in the current generation has managed to reproduce the delicate flavor of Aunt Mary's.

Time does appear to stand still here—but time has run out for all of us, and today we are packing our memories along with the mementos. My son is now a college "man" and he will help carry out the boxes.

What a special privilege he has had. Within the same walls where his father spent happy growing-up years—untold Christmases and Fourths of July—he has enjoyed a childhood. One Christmas, for example, he was given a game that had been his dad's many years before. I think that was the same year his father received his grandfather's silver penknife.

Among my most precious memories are the hours spent talking about family things like the cracker bowl that was brought from England and for years has been a cache for Mary's rose petals, ones from her wedding bouquet and when her daughter was born. From time to time, we have taken the perfectly pressed linens from her drawers and recounted their stories. Some stitched by namesakes, some meant for hope chests and never used, some great-great-grandmother's. My favorites are three doilies I have borrowed over the years—they are mine to treasure now. So much of the texture of my life is a rose stitched by a great-grandmother from thread too delicate to imagine. It means more than faded faces in the album.

I am glad that I have listened. I am happy for every moment in this citadel of family pride. And while sadness fills my heart, when we no longer return to this tree-shaded boulevard I will look at the motifs on my linens—birds, butterflies, flowers—and remember with pleasure calm, cool yesterdays in this special home.

Jenny Walton

I long to put the experience of fifty years at once into your young lives, to give you at once the key of that treasure chamber every gem of which has cost me tears and struggles and prayers, but you must work for these inward treasures yourselves.

Harriet Beecher Stowe
to her twin daughters, 1861

LEGACY

I, who was never quite sure

About being a girl, needed another

life, and another image to remind me . . .

I made you to find me.

Anne Sexton
The Double Image

You I'll reward first
for the moments of your births,
those three brief instants
when I understood my life.

But wisdom bends as light does
around the objects it touches.
The only legacy you need was left
by accident long ago:
a secret in the genes.
The rest is small change.

Linda Pastan
Last Will

Victoria

THE SEMPSTRESS

'Do you mean to say your daughter is nine years old,' said a friend, 'and she doesn't know how to sew? She really must learn to sew. In bad weather sewing is a better occupation for a child of that age than reading story books.'

'Nine years old? And she can't sew?' said another friend. 'When she was eight, my daughter embroidered this tray cloth for me, look at it . . . Oh! I don't say it's fine needlework, but it's nicely done all the same. Nowadays my daughter cuts out her own underclothes. I can't bear anyone in my house to mend holes with pins!'

I meekly poured all this domestic wisdom over Bel-Gazou.

'You're nine years old and you don't know how to sew? You really must learn to sew . . .'

Flouting truth, I even added:

'When I was eight years old, I remember I embroidered a tray cloth . . .

Oh! It wasn't fine needlework, I dare say . . . And then, in bad weather . . .'

She has therefore learned to sew. And although—with one bare sunburnt leg tucked beneath her, and her body at ease in its bathing suit—she looks more like a fisherboy mending a net than an industrious little girl, she seems to experience no boyish repugnance. Her hands, stained the colour of tobacco-juice by sun and sea, hem in a way that seems against nature; their version of the simple running stitch resembles the zigzag dotted lines of the a road map, but she buttonholes and scallops with elegance and is severely critical of the embroidery of others.

She sews and kindly keeps me company if rain blurs the horizon of the sea. She also sews during the torrid hour when the spindle bushes gather their circles of shadow directly under them. Moreover, it sometime happens that a quarter of an hour before dinner, black

in her white dress—'Bel-Gazou! your hands and frock are clean, and don't forget it!'—she sits solemnly down with a square of material between her fingers. Then my friends applaud: 'Just look at her! Isn't she good? That's right! Your mother must be pleased!'

Her mother says nothing—great joys must be controlled. But ought one to feign them? I shall speak the truth: I don't much like my daughter sewing.

When she reads, she returns all bewildered and with flaming cheeks, from the island where the chest full of precious stones is hidden, from the dismal castle where a fair-haired orphan child is persecuted. She is soaking up a tested and time-honoured poison, whose effects have long been familiar. If she draws, or colours pictures, a semi-articulate song issues from her, unceasing as the hum of bees round the privet. It is the same as the buzzing of flies as they work, the slow waltz of the house-painter, the

refrain of the spinner at her wheel. But Bel-Gazou is silent when she sews, silent for hours on end, with her mouth firmly closed, concealing her large, new-cut incisors that bite into the moist heart of a fruit like little saw-edge blades. She is silent, and she—why not write down the word that frightens me—she is thinking.

A new evil? A torment that I had not foreseen? Sitting in a grassy dell, or half buried in hot sand and gazing out to sea, she is thinking, as well I know. She thinks rapidly when she is listening, with a well-bred pretence of discretion, to remarks imprudently exchanged above her head. But it would seem that with this needle-play she has discovered the perfect means of adventuring, stitch by stitch, point by point, along a road of risks and temptations. Silence . . . the hand armed with the steel dart moves back and forth. Nothing will stop the unchecked little explorer. At what mo-

ment must I utter the 'Halt!' that will brutally arrest her in full flight? Oh, for those young embroiderers of bygone days, sitting on a hard little stool in the shelter of their mother's ample skirts! Maternal authority kept them there for years and years, never rising except to change the skein of silk, or to elope with a stranger. Think of Philomène de Watteville and her canvas on which she embroidered the loss and the despair of Albert Savarus . . .

'What are you thinking about, Bel-Gazou?'

'Nothing, mother. I'm counting my stitches.'

Silence. The needle pierces the material. A coarse trail of chain-stitch follows very unevenly in its wake. Silence . . .

'Mother?'

'Darling?'

'Is it only when people are married that a man can put his arm round a

lady's waist?'

'Yes . . . No . . . It depends. If they are very good friends and have known each other a long time, you understand . . . As I said before: it depends. Why do you want to know?'

'For no particular reason, mother.'

Two stitches, ten misshapen chain-stitches.

'Mother? Is Madame X married?'

'She has been. She is divorced.'

'I see. And Monsieur F, is he married?'

'Why, of course he is; you know that.'

'Oh! Yes . . . Then it's all right if one of the two is married?'

'What is all right?'

'To depend.'

'One doesn't say: "To depend." '

'But you said just now that it depended.'

'But what has it got to do with you? Is it any concern of yours?'

'No, mother.'

I let it drop. I feel inadequate, self-conscious, displeased with myself. I should have answered differently and I could not think what to say.

Bel-Gazou also drops the subject; she sews. But she pays little attention to her sewing, overlaying it with pictures, associations of names and people, all the results of patient observation. A little later will come other curiosities, other questions, and especially other silences. Would to God that Bel-Gazou were the bewildered and simple child who questions crudely, open-eyed! But she is too near the truth, and too natural not to know as a birthright, that all nature hestitates before that most majestic and most disturbing of instincts, and that it is wise to tremble, to be silent and to lie when one draws near to it.

Colette
My Mother's House

In fact, [Mother] was a sweet eccentric, the only middle-class woman I have ever known who had not rejected the middle class—that would have been an act of will—but had skipped it altogether. She liked a simple life and simple people, and would have been happier, I think, if she had stayed in the backlands of Alabama riding wild on the horses she so often talked about, not so lifelong lonely for the black men and women who had taught her the only religion she ever knew. I didn't know what she was saying when she moved her lips in a Baptist church or a Catholic cathedral or, less often, in a synagogue, but it was obvious that God could be found anywhere, because several times a week we would stop in a church, any church, and she seemed to be at home in all of them.

Lillian Hellman
An Unfinished Woman

My mother . . . liked reading her Bible in her own rocking chair, and while she rocked. She considered herself something of a student. "Run get me my Concordance," she'd say, referring to a little book bound in thin leather, falling apart. She liked to correct herself. Then from time to time her lips would twitch in the stern books of the Bible, such as Romans, providing her as they did with memories of her Grandfather Carden who had been a Baptist preacher in the days when she grew up in West Virginia. She liked to try in retrospect to correct Grandpa too . . . I'm grateful that, from my mother's example, . . . I had found a love of sitting and reading the Bible for myself and looking things up in it.

Eudora Welty
One Writer's Beginnings

11 October 1912

A happy birthday to you, dearest Mother, and many, many returns of the day! How good it is to think of you visiting us again. It means that you will be there to see something of my new and larger work. Whatever success comes to me seems incomplete because you are so often not at my side to be glad with me. But now you will have a chance to realize more fully into what new worlds of thought, feeling and aspiration I am entering, and see what new and fascinating fields of knowledge and action are opening before me. This visit in Washington is truly a flood of fresh experiences, impressions and observations, and it is only a foretaste of what I am likely to have in the near future . . .

Your affectionate child,

Helen Keller

To her daughter, Madame de Grignan

Livry, Holy Wednesday, March 25th, 1671

I have been here three hours, my dear child . . . I am supposed to be in retreat . . . But what I shall do . . . is to think of you, my child.

There is no place, no spot,—either in the house or in the church, in the country or in the garden,—where I have not seen you . . . But in vain I turn—in vain I seek: that dear child whom I passionately love is two hundred leagues distant from me. I have her no more; and then I weep, and cannot cease. My love that is weakness; but as for me, I do not know how to be strong against a feeling so powerful and so natural.

I cannot tell in what frame of mind you will be when reading this letter: perhaps chance may bring it to you inopportunely, and it may not read in the spirit in which it is written,—but for that there is no remedy. To write it, at least, consoles me now; that is all I ask of it at present, for the state into which this place has thrown me is inconceivable. Do not speak of my weaknesses; but you must love and respect my tears, since they proceed from a heart which is wholly yours.

Madame de Sévigné

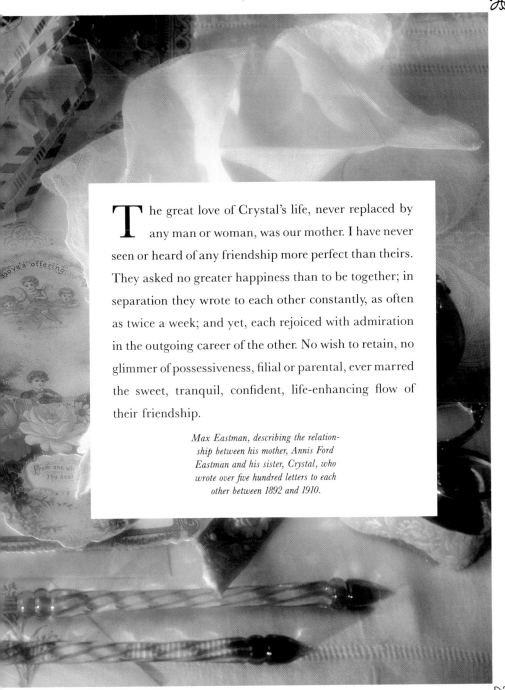

The great love of Crystal's life, never replaced by any man or woman, was our mother. I have never seen or heard of any friendship more perfect than theirs. They asked no greater happiness than to be together; in separation they wrote to each other constantly, as often as twice a week; and yet, each rejoiced with admiration in the outgoing career of the other. No wish to retain, no glimmer of possessiveness, filial or parental, ever marred the sweet, tranquil, confident, life-enhancing flow of their friendship.

Max Eastman, describing the relationship between his mother, Annis Ford Eastman and his sister, Crystal, who wrote over five hundred letters to each other between 1892 and 1910.

I had been apt enough to learn, and willing enough, when my mother and I lived alone together. I can faintly remember learning the alphabet at her knee. To this day, when I look upon the fat black letters in the primer, the puzzling novelty of their shapes, and the easy good-nature of O and Q and S, seem to present themselves again before me as they used to . . . I seemed to have walked along a patch of flowers as far as the crocodile-book, and to have been cheered by the gentleness of my mother's voice and manner all the way.

Charles Dickens
David Copperfield

There is no Frigate like a Book
To take us Lands away
Nor any Coursers like a Page
Of prancing Poetry—
This Traverse may the poorest take
Without oppress of Toll—
How frugal is the Chariot
That bears the Human Soul!

Emily Dickinson
No. 1263

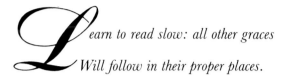

Learn to read slow: all other graces
Will follow in their proper places.

William Walker
The Art of Reading

Reading List for My Children

_____

_____

_____

_____

_____

_____

_____

_____

_____

_____

_____

_____

_____

_____

_____

A MOTHER'S AMBITIONS

"I want my daughters to be beautiful, accomplished, and good; to be admired, loved, and respected; to have a happy youth, to be well and wisely married, and to lead useful, pleasant lives, with as little care and sorrow to try them as God sees fit to send. To be loved and chosen by a good man is the best and sweetest thing which can happen to a woman; and I sincerely hope my girls may know this beautiful experience. It is natural to think of it, Meg; right to hope and wait for it, and wise to prepare for it; so that, when the happy time comes, you may feel ready for the duties and worthy of the joy. My dear girls, I *am* ambitious for you, but not to have you make a dash in the world,—marry rich men merely because they are rich, or have splendid houses, which are not homes because love is wanting. Money is a needful and precious thing,—and, when used well, a noble thing,—but I never want you to think it is the first or only prize to strive for. I'd rather see you poor men's wives, if you were happy, beloved, contented, than queens on thrones, without self-respect and peace."

"Poor girls don't stand any chance, Belle says, unless they put themselves forward," sighed Meg.

"Then we'll be old maids," said Jo stoutly.

"Right, Jo; better be happy old maids than unhappy wives or unmaidenly girls, running about to find husbands," said Mrs. March decidedly. "Don't be troubled, Meg; poverty seldom daunts a sincere lover. Some of the best and most honored women I know were poor girls, but so love-worthy that they were not allowed to be old maids. Leave these things to time; make this home happy, so that you may be fit for homes of your own, if they are offered you, and contented here if they are not. One thing remember, my girls: mother is always ready to be your confidant, father to be your friend; and both of us trust and hope that our daughters, whether married or single, will be the pride and comfort of our lives."

"We will, Marmee, we will!" cried both, with all their hearts, as she bade them good-night.

Louisa May Alcott
Little Women

My mother liked to sing, but she would wait until my father wasn't around because he would correct her pitch and straighten her posture and insist she use her lungs and diaphragm better. . . .

At night with the lights out, after she had heard our prayers, my mother would sing to James and me, and we thought she was great. She'd sing "Down by the Old Mill Stream" or some Cole Porter hit she knew from college. She loved Frank Sinatra. She would stand by our bed, crooning imitations into one of the bedposts as if it were a microphone, and afterward we would clap in the dark until our hands stung. (At the end of "Pennies from Heaven," she would place a penny on each post for us to find in the morning.) "Thank you, thank you," she would whisper with a low, wonderful laugh, smiling and bending over us to wetly kiss our cheeks, her hair down, long, black, and sweeping against my chest and chin, smelling soapy and dry. And if the moon was out it lit up the lake, and the lake light shone into the room through the slats of the blinds, tentatively striping her hair and face or the arm of her sweater. And as she moved—to kiss James, to tuck in the blankets—the stripes moved up and down with her. When she left she always kept the door slightly unlatched, the lamp from the hall framing the door in cracks of light interrupted only by hinges. She always called in a whisper, "Good night my sweet sparrows". . . .

Lorrie Moore
What Is Seized

If it had not been for my mother's conviction and determination that music was my destiny, it is quite conceivable that I would have become a carpenter.

Pablo Casals

Forgotten mornings when he walked

with his mother

Through the parables

Of sunlight

And the legend of the green chapels.

Dylan Thomas
Poem in October

SHARED MOMENTS

True happiness is of a retired nature,
and an enemy to pomp and noise; it
arises, in the first place, from the enjoy-
ment of one's self; and, in the next, from
the friendship and conversation of a few
select companions.

Joseph Addison
The Spectator

One summer, in Le Pouliguen, on the Atlantic coast, we became shrimp saviors. I had caught three shrimps and a little crab. That evening we put a pailful of sea water on the bedroom mantel in our *pension de famille*; and my mother settled down in bed with a book. She was not one of those ladies who put their children to bed and then go out dancing. I began to cry, and explained that I wanted to put my three shrimps and the crab back into the sea. She dressed me in my rompers, and we took the pail and emptied the contents into the harbour. I was blissfully happy . . . and she was too.

Simone Signoret
Nostalgia Isn't What It Used to Be

Family Vacations

*M*rs. Sedley, you may be sure, clasped her daughter to her heart with all maternal eagerness and affection, running out of the door as the carriage drew up before the little garden gate, to welcome the weeping, trembling bride . . .

How the floodgates were opened, and mother and daughter wept, when they were together embracing each other in this sanctuary, may readily be imagined by every reader who possesses the least sentimental turn. When don't ladies weep? At what occasion of joy, sorrow, or other business of life? and, after such an event as a marriage, mother and daughter were surely at liberty to give way to a sensibility which is as tender as it is refreshing. About a question of marriage I have seen women who hate each other kiss and cry together quite fondly. How much more do they feel when they love! Good mothers are married over again at their daughters' weddings: and as for subsequent events, who does not know how ultra-maternal grandmothers are?—in fact a woman, until she is a grandmother, does not often really know what to be a mother is.

William Makepeace Thackeray
Vanity Fair

Wedding Day Memories

THE HEART OF
A SPECIAL THANKSGIVING

*I*t did snow that Thanksgiving. And we did go to grandmother's house. But as we made our way through the snow, it was not a dapple-gray that guided us; rather we drove in a drafty little English sports car, along the Eastern Seaboard. Every so often, a gust of wind blew the snow through the canvas side curtains, dusting our clothes like powdered sugar.

My grandmother lived in Connecticut, I in Washington, and I had invited a young naval officer to spend Thanksgiving with us. I was sure my Nebraska-raised grandmother would welcome a fellow midwesterner stranded for the holiday.

When we arrived, like waifs in the storm, our feet nearly frozen, my grandmother settled my friend in an upstairs bedroom, tucking him under the eaves amidst rose-patterned wallpaper and piles of handmade quilts. From the first moment, her clear blue eyes gazed on him approvingly; she was not very approving of his tiny car, however.

Our Thanksgiving guest had never been to Connecticut before, and he was charmed by the coziness of the landscape. Iowa, he told me, was very different save for the northeastern corner, where he had grown up the son of a county-seat newspaper editor. There dairy farms were nestled in rolling hills, somewhat like those in the Connecticut countryside.

There is no need to dwell on his joy in my grandmother's cooking. And though I am sure he missed his mother's table, he relished every meal, all of us lingering comfortably over cups of coffee. He and my grandmother often seemed transported as they talked about familiar places and memories. I remember thinking, if I look out the window now, I will be on a snow-bound open prairie and not in a sleepy New England town.

It was surprising to me how little I knew about this quiet Iowan who was then a casual friend. But on long walks across the stone bridge and along the green and chatting in my grandmother's parlor, I began to see how much he reminded me of her in his midwestern wit and disarming presence.

At Christmas he took the train to Iowa; and I returned to Connecticut, missing my cordial companion but not his silly car. My grandmother chose this occasion to give me the diamond earrings she had worn for a half-century, realizing before I did that Thanksgiving had been a new beginning for me. I wore them for the first time the next July on my wedding day. They did not sparkle nearly as brightly as my grandmother's knowing eyes.

Jenny Walton

LONG AGO TREE

My mother had a Christmas tree,
But it was not like mine;
It had no lovely glowing balls,
Electric lights to shine;
It hadn't any tinsel bands,
That little tree she had,
Or shining silver icicles,
Or stars to make it glad!

But there were lights on mother's tree,
For there were candles there,
All flickering in the branches green,
And spicing all the air;

And there were puffy popcorn ropes,
With cranberries between,
And oranges, and apples bright,
And cookies to be seen!

I wish that I had been there then,
To sniff the candle smell,
To see the snow-white popcorn ropes,
The oranges as well!
My mother would be standing there,
Aquiver with surprise—
A little girl in funny clothes,
With starlight in her eyes!

Christmas Traditions

discovered when I had a child of my own that I had become a biased observer of small children. Instead of looking at them with affectionate but nonpartisan eyes, I saw each of them as older or younger, bigger or smaller, more or less graceful, intelligent, or skilled than my own child. This troubled me. I felt that I had learned a great deal about mothers by being one, but that I had become in some way a less objective observer of children.

Margaret Mead
Blackberry Winter

*D*uring the years I was in elementary school, there were a series of arrangements for my care when [Mother] was busy or out of town, afternoons spent with school mates, from whose houses I would be picked up at five or six, weekends spent at Aunt Marie's. If I was sick, the effort to have someone available besides the maid usually meant calling on Liza, my mother's sister, who was a public-school art teacher and could come in the afternoon, bringing watercolors and a jaunty sense of wildness, eccentric clothing, tales of artists and of hours spent on picket lines, and echoes of a household that when I visited was full of siren disorder, public quarrelling and four-letter words, and newly painted murals in the bathroom. Only when I began trying to combine motherhood and housekeeping with professional work myself did I begin to get a sense of the complex infrastructure of my mother's life, the number of people involved in looking after me in the afternoons, getting me home, coming over to cook dinner and of the way in which my life has been enriched by the diversity of these arrangements and the different kinds of people with whom my life was linked.

Mary Catherine Bateson
With a Daughter's Eye:
A Memoir of Margaret Mead and Gregory Bateson

The shadow of my mother danced around the room

to a tune that my shadow sang . . .

Jamaica Kincaid
"My Mother"

GENERATIONS

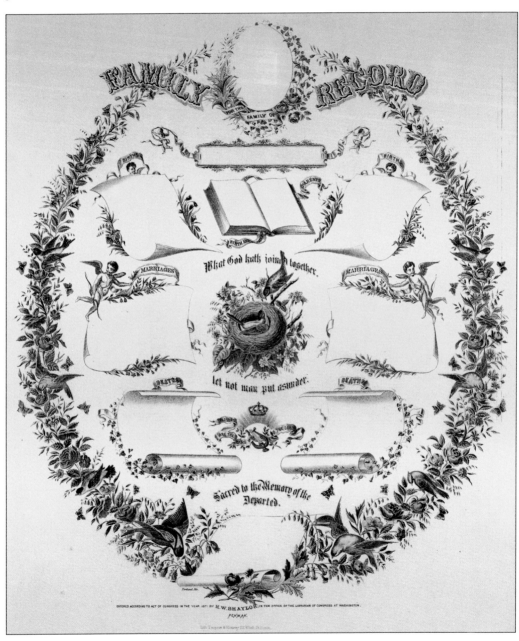

*B*road-streeted Richmond . . .

The trees in the streets are old trees used to living with people,

Family trees that remember your grandfather's name.

Stephen Vincent Benet
John Brown's Body

Registry of Family Heirlooms

SIGNIFICANT MOMENTS
IN THE LIFE OF MY MOTHER

There are some stories which my mother does not tell when there are men present: never at dinner, never at parties. She tells them to women only, usually in the kitchen, when they or we are helping with the dishes or shelling peas, or taking the tops and tails off the string beans, or husking corn. She tells them in a lowered voice, without moving her hands around in the air, and they contain no sound effects. These are stories of romantic betrayals, unwanted pregnancies, illnesses of various horrible kinds, marital infidelities, mental break-downs, tragic suicides, unpleasant lingering deaths. They are not rich in detail or embroidered with incident: they are stark and factual. The women, their own hands moving among the dirty dishes or the husks of vegetables, nod solemnly.

Some of these stories, it is understood, are not to be passed on to my father, because they would upset him. It is well known that women can deal with this sort of thing better than men can. Men are not to be told anything they might find too painful; the secret depths of human nature, the sordid physicalities, might overwhelm or damage them. For instance, men often faint at the sight of their own blood, to which they are not accustomed. For this reason you should never stand behind one in the line at the Red Cross donor clinic. Men, for some mysterious reason, find life more difficult than women do. (My mother believes this, despite the female bodies, trapped, diseased, disappearing, or abandoned, that litter her stories.) Men must be allowed to play in the sandbox of their choice, as happily as they can, without disturbance; otherwise they get cranky and won't eat their dinners. There are all kinds of things that men are simply not equipped to understand, so why expect it of them? Not everyone shares this belief about men; nevertheless, it has its uses.

'She dug up the shrubs from around the house,' says my mother. This story is about a shattered marriage: serious business. My mother's eyes widen. The other women lean forward. 'All she left him were the shower curtains.' There is a collective sigh, an expelling of breath. My father enters the kitchen, wondering when the tea will be ready, and the women close ranks, turning to him their deceptive blankly smiling faces. Soon afterwards, my mother emerges from the kitchen, carrying the tea pot, and sets it down on the table in its ritual place. . . .

'In my next incarnation,' my mother said once, 'I'm going to be an archaeologist and go around digging things up.' We were sitting on the bed that had once been my brother's, then mine, then my sister's; we were sorting out things from one of the trunks, deciding what could now be given away or thrown out. My mother believes that what you save from the past is mostly a matter of choice.

At that time something wasn't right in the family; someone wasn't happy. My mother was angry: her good cheer was not paying off.

This statement of hers startled me. It was the first time I'd ever heard my mother say that she might have wanted to be something other than what she was. I must have been thirty-five at the time, but it was still shocking and slightly offensive to me to learn that my mother might not have been totally contented fulfilling the role in which fate had cast her: that of being my mother. What thumbsuckers we all are, I thought, when it comes to mothers.

Shortly after this I became a mother myself, and this moment altered for me.

Margaret Atwood

"Remember" is always a magic word, but especially when mother and daughter use it. Years ago they saw the same thing—or, rather, the same event happened before their eyes—and now, twenty years later, they discovered that each saw something entirely different from the other. The mother tells her story; the daughter tells. What each saw is unbelievable. What each missed in unbelievable. Put the two stories together, and there, perhaps, is the real event. But who can say what the real event is?

Jessamyn West
Mother's Day

*T*he harder little Leo tried to remember his mother, the more she eluded him. He tried to identify her by questioning those who had known her, but in vain. They told him she was good, gentle, upright, proud, intelligent, and an excellent storyteller, but he could not attach a face to this assortment of qualities, and as though to deepen the mystery, there was not a single portrait of her in the house. Only a silhouette cut out of black paper, showing her at the age of ten or twelve, with a round forehead and a round chin, her hair in a veil at the nape of her neck. His whole life long Leo Tolstoy tried to instill life into this frustrating profile. He grew older, but his mother remained a little girl.

Henri Troyat
Tolstoy

I go searching for her.

My first memories of her are early, and are memories of smell, that oft-neglected sense, which is perhaps the first sense we use fully. Mother always smelled beautiful. I remember burrowing into her neck just for the soft loveliness of scented skin.

After smell came sound, the sound of her voice, singing to me, talking. I took the beauty of her voice for granted until I was almost grown up.

Scent. Sound. Vision.

I remember going into her room just before dinner, when she was sitting at her dressing table, rubbing sweet-smelling creams and lotions into her face. She had a set of ivory rollers from Paris, which I liked to play with; and a silver-backed nail buffer. Sometimes she let me buff my own nails until they were a pearly pink. The cake of French rouge, and the buffing, makes for a much prettier nail than lacquer.

I watched her brush her hair, a dark mahogany with red glints, thick and wavy, with a deep widow's peak. On the bed her evening dress was laid out; I remember one of flowered chiffon, short in front and long in back, that short-lived style of the twenties. Her shoes were bronze kid, and as tiny as Cinderella's. . . .

Once when Mother and I were in New York, during a college vacation, we had lunch together in a pleasant downtown restaurant before going to the theatre, and I remember, with the same clarity with which I remember the little embroidered dress, that I leaned across the table and said, "Oh, Mother, it's such *fun* to be with you!" And it was. We enjoyed things together, the theatre, museums, music, food, conversation.

When I was pregnant with Josephine I told Mother, "All I could possibly hope for with children is that they love me as much as I love you."

Josephine, when she was five or six years old, lightened my heart one evening when she flung her arms around me and said, "Oh, Mama, you're so *exciting!*" What more glorious compliment could a child give a parent? My parents were exciting to me, but their lives were far more glamorous than mine. When Jo made that lovely, spontaneous remark I felt anything but exciting; I was in the midst of a difficult decade of literary rejection, of struggling with small children and a large house; and that remark of Jo's restored my faith in myself, both as a writer and as a mother. Even though I knew I might never again be published; even though I could not see any end to the physical struggle and perpetual fatigue, Josephine helped heal doubt. It is a risky business to hope, but my daughter gave me the courage to take the risk.

I wonder if I ever, unknowingly, gave my mother like courage? I am well aware of all the things I have done which have distressed her, but perhaps simply the fact that I have always loved her may sometimes have helped.

Madeleine L'Engle
The Summer of the
Great-Grandmother

THE DIRTY-BILLED
FREEZE FOOTY

Remember that Saturday morning
Mother forgot the word gull?

We were all awake but still in bed
and she called out, "Hey kids!
What's the name of that bird that eats garbage
and stands around in cold water on the beach?"

And you, the quick one, the youngest daughter
piped right back: "A dirty-billed freeze footy!"

And she laughed till she was weak,
until it hurt her. And you had done it:
reduced our queen to warm and helpless rubble.

And the rest of the day, baking or cleaning
or washing out hair until it squeaked,

whenever she caught sight of you
it would start all over again.

Judith Hemschemeyer
Very Close and Very Slow

I always found my mother's attitude to me curiously disconcerting. She seemed to find most of the things I did slightly comic ("killing" was the word she most often used). Long after my father had died I rang her up to tell her that I had been asked to go to some distant town to sit as a Judge, hoping she might be impressed. "*You*, a Judge?" She started to giggle. "*You*? Whatever do they think they're doing, asking *you* to be a Judge?" and then she laughed so much that she had to put down the telephone receiver. From time to time she seemed to find it hard to remember essential things about me, such as whether I took sugar, or my name. In later years, she often looked at me vaguely and called me "Daisy," which was my aunt's name. Not until she was very old did I find some short stories which she had written, which showed her concern about me and her anxiety, no doubt entirely justified, about what I got up to when out of her sight.

John Mortimer
Clinging to the Wreckage

THE AGE OF MAKE-BELIEVE

Running eagerly to the door, the child glanced back too soon, and saw her mother, for one instant of blighting reality, with the artificial cheerfulness wiped away from her face. While Mrs. Archbald sank down into her easy chair, her released mind sprang back from the severe strain of keeping up an appearance. Not her duty alone, but love, life, the world, the universe, God,—all these had become suddenly too much for her. Stripped of her pleasant smile, stripped even of her sunny disposition, she was only a tired middle-aged woman, who rested, for one precious hour, from the wearing endeavour to look on the bright side of things and hope for the best.

"Mamma, dear, don't you wish you were going?"

"No, darling." Mrs. Archbald's voice was faint but encouraging. "All I ask is a good night's sleep and a soft bed to enjoy it in."

Stabbed by this new vision of her mother, Jenny Blair whirled round in her party dress, and darting across the room, flung herself sobbing upon Mrs. Archbald's knees. "Oh, Mamma! Oh, Mamma, I've never seen you before!"

"My dear child! My darling child, what is the matter?" Clasping her tenderly but carefully, lest she should rumple the flounces of Swiss muslin, Mrs. Archbald tried to look in her daughter's face. "Have you a pain anywhere? Is your sash tied too tight?"

"Oh, I don't know. I don't know. But I've never seen you before."

"Why, Jenny Blair, how absurd!"

"I've never seen you before, but I love you, Mamma. I love you more than anything in the world."

"My precious child!" Almost sobbing in her turn, for she was genuinely moved in spite of her sentimental evasion, Mrs. Archbald forgot the flounces and the blue sash while she gathered her child to her bosom. "There, there. Mamma knows you love her. There is nothing to cry about."

"I wish you were going, Mamma. I don't want to go and leave you at home."

"But I'd rather be at home, dear. I haven't the strength to stand anything more after helping you and your aunts to dress. Poor Aunt Etta had another bad dream last night, and I had to sit up. Are you perfectly sure you don't feel a pain inside? I hope," she added gravely, "you haven't eaten anything I told you not to."

"It isn't that, Mamma. Oh, it isn't that."

"Then what is it? Has anybody hurt your feelings? You must remember that Aunt Etta is very nervous and sometimes she speaks more sharply than she means to."

"No, it isn't that. Nobody has said anything."

"Well, if there is nothing really the matter, you'd better run on and not keep your grandfather waiting. Mrs. Peyton promised to send you home early in the morning, and then you can tell me about the party."

"Oh, yes, I'll tell you about it." Love and sadness melted together and vanished. Immediately, Jenny Blair began to live in the hope of coming back, primed with news, to describe the evening to her mother. "I'll remember everything that happens, Mamma, and I'll bring you some of the little cakes with pink roses in icing."

Ellen Glasgow
The Sheltered Life

PHOTOGRAPHS AND MEMORIES

*T*he rooms in our house were like songs. Each had its own rhythmic spacing and clutter, which if you crossed your eyes became a sort of musical notation, a score—clusters of eighth notes, piles of triplets, and the wooden roundness of doorways, like clefs, all blending in a kind of concerto. Or sometimes, as with the bathroom, with its motif of daisies and red plastic, they created a sort of jingle, something small, likeable, functional. It was the bookcase in the living room that seemed particularly symphonic, the books all friendly with one another, a huge chorus of them in a hum; they stood packed behind glass doors with loose metal knobs. My mother also kept photo albums, scrap-books, yearbooks on the bottom shelf of the case, along with the big, heavy books like *Smith's World History* and the *Golden Treasury of Children's Stories*. In one book she had black and white pictures of herself, starting from when she was little. Gray, empty days I would take that book out and look at it. By the time I was nine, I knew all the pictures by heart. To stare at them, to know those glimpses, I felt, was to know her, to become her, to make my mother a woman with adventures, a woman in a story, a book, a movie. The photos somehow seemed powerful. Sometimes I still look at them, with a cup of coffee, with the television on.

Lorrie Moore
What Is Seized

133

Not-To-Be-Forgotten Family Stories

ALICE'S EVIDENCE

*W*ake up, Alice dear!" said her sister. "Why, what a long sleep you've had!"

"Oh, I've had such a curious dream!" said Alice. And she told her sister, as well as she could remember them, all these strange Adventures of hers that you have just been reading about; and, when she had finished, her sister kissed her, and said, "It *was* a curious dream, dear, certainly; but now run in to your tea: it's getting late." So Alice got up and ran off, thinking while she ran, as well she might, what a wonderful dream it had been.

But her sister sat still just as she left her, leaning her head on her hand, watching the setting sun, and thinking of little Alice and all her wonderful Adventures.

. . . She pictured to herself how this same little sister of hers would, in the after-time, be herself a grown woman; and how she would keep, through all her riper years, the simple and loving heart of her childhood; and how she would gather about her other little children, and make *their* eyes bright and eager with many a strange tale, perhaps even with the dream of Wonderland of long ago; and how she would feel with all their simple sorrows, and find a pleasure in all their simple joys, remembering her own child-life, and the happy summer days.

Lewis Carroll
Alice's Adventures
in Wonderland

Ritz Hastings 147 TREMONT STREET, BOSTON MASS.

MY GRANDMOTHER'S
LOVE LETTERS

There are no stars to-night
But those of memory.
Yet how much room for memory there is
In the loose girdle of soft rain.

There is even room enough
For the letters of my mother's mother,
Elizabeth,
That have been pressed so long
Into a corner of the roof
That they are brown and soft,
And liable to melt as snow.

Over the greatness of such space
Steps must be gentle.
It is all hung by an invisible white hair.
It trembles as birch limbs webbing the air.

And I ask myself:

"Are your fingers long enough to play
Old keys that are but echoes:
Is the silence strong enough
To carry back the music to its source
And back to you again
As though to her?"

Yet I would lead my grandmother
    by the hand
Through much of what
    she would not understand;
And so I stumble.
And the rain continues on the roof
With such a sound of gently pitying laughter.

Hart Crane
The Complete Poems and Selected
Letters and Prose of Hart Crane

PERMISSIONS AND PHOTO CREDITS

COVER

Photograph by Jim Hedrich.

INTRODUCTION

7: Photograph by Katrina. Dried flower collage by Sandy Puckett.

MOTHER'S GIFTS

9: Photograph by Jim Hedrich.

10: Excerpt from *My Family and Other Animals* by Gerald Durrell. Copyright © 1956 by Gerald Durrell. Reprinted with permission of Curtis Brown Ltd. on behalf of Gerald Durrell.

11: Photograph by Jeff McNamara.

12: "Maternal Caress," 1891, by Mary Cassatt (American, 1845–1926) is from The Baltimore Museum of Art: Estate of Mrs. Q. A. Shaw McKean, BMA 1953.118.

14: Photograph by Keith Scott Morton. Excerpt from *Remembrance of Things Past, Volume One: Swann's Way and Within A Budding Grove*, by Marcel Proust, translated by C.K. Scott Moncrieff and Terence Kilmartin. Copyright © 1981 by Random House, Inc. and Chatto & Windus. Reprinted by permission of Random House, Inc.

15: Wedding portrait of Rosa Walton Bennison, 1895. Excerpt by Adele Kanaley Miller Christensen from *My Mother Before Me*. Copyright © 1986 by Julie Kettle Gundlach. Published by arrangement with Carol Publishing Group.

16: Photograph by Monica Roberts.

17: Photograph by Michael Grimm. Excerpt from *Memoirs of a Dutiful Daughter* by Simone de Beauvoir. Published by Editions Gallimard. Reprinted by permission of Harper & Row, Publishers, Inc.

18–19: Photograph by Toshi Otsuki. Excerpt from *The State of Stony Lonesome* by Jessamyn West. Copyright © 1984 by the Estate of Jessamyn West McPherson. Reprinted by permission of Harcourt Brace Jovanovich, Inc.

20: Excerpt from *My Mother Before Me*. Copyright © 1986 by Julie Kettle Gundlach. Published by arrangement with Carol Publishing Group.

21: Photograph by William P. Steele.

22: Photograph by Tina Mucci.

23: Excerpt from *The Adversary* by Phyllis McGinley, 1960.

50: Photograph by Steve Gross.

51: Excerpt from *Go Tell It On The Mountain* by James Baldwin. Copyright © 1952, 1953 by James Baldwin. Used by permission of Doubleday, a division of Bantam, Doubleday, Dell Publishing Group.

52–54: Painting by Christine Merrill. Excerpt from "A Dog's Tale" by Mark Twain is reprinted from *The Complete Short Stories of Mark Twain.* Copyright © 1903 by Samuel L. Clemens. Published by Bantam, Doubleday, Dell Publishing Group.

55: Photograph by Starr Ockenga.

57: Photograph from *Images of America: A Panorama of History in Photographs*, Smithsonian Books, 1989.

58: "My Mother" by Ann Taylor is from *Original Poems for Infant Minds*, 1804.

59: Photograph by Jim Hedrich. "The Joys of Being Sick in Bed" is from *From My Mother's Kitchen* by Mimi Sheraton. Copyright © 1979 by Mimi Sheraton. Reprinted by permission of Harper & Row, Publishers, Inc.

60: Photograph by Jim Hedrich.

61: Photograph by Bryan E. McCay.

62–63: Photographs by Elyse Lewin. "A Grandmother's Ritual" by Sylvia Thompson originally appeared in the November, 1989, issue of *Victoria.*

64: Photograph by Tina Mucci. "A Cooking House" is from *From My Mother's Kitchen* by Mimi Sheraton. Copyright © 1979 by Mimi Sheraton. Reprinted by permission of Harper & Row, Publishers, Inc.

66: Photograph by John E. Kane. Background photograph by William P. Steele.

68: Photograph by Toshi Otsuki.

69: Photograph by Chris Mead. Excerpt from "Mother's Day" in *Crimson Ramblers of the World, Farewell*, copyright © 1970 by Jessamyn West, reprinted by permission of Harcourt Brace Jovanovich, Inc.

71: Photograph by William P. Steele. Excerpt from "The Fragrant Path" by Louise Beebe Wilder. Copyright © 1932. Reprinted in *The American Gardener.*

72: Photograph by Keith Scott Morton.

73: Photograph by Carin Krasner.

74: Photograph by Jim Hedrich. "A Family Home" by Jenny Walton originally appeared in the August, 1988 issue of *Victoria.*

L E G A C Y

77:   Photograph by Jim Hedrich.

78:   Photograph by Toshi Otsuki.

79:   "Last Will" by Linda Pastan is from *A Fraction of Darkness: Poems by Linda Pastan*. Copyright © 1985 by Linda Pastan. Reprinted by permission of the author and W.W. Norton & Company, Inc.

80:   Photograph by Katrina. "The Sempstress" by Colette is from *My Mother's House*, translated by Una Vincenzo Troubridge and Ed McLeod and *Sido*, translated by Ed McLeod. Copyright © 1953 by Colette. Reprinted by permission of Secker and Warburg Ltd.

81:   Photograph by Toshi Otsuki.

82:   Photograph by Starr Ockenga.

83:   Photograph by Tria Giovan.

84:   Photograph by Chris Mead. Excerpt from *An Unfinished Woman* by Lillian Hellman. Copyright © 1969 by Lillian Hellman. Reprinted with permission of Little, Brown and Company.

85:   Photograph by Monica Roberts. Excerpt from *One Writer's Beginnings* by Eudora Welty. Copyright © 1983 by Eudora Welty. Published by Harvard University Press.

86:   Photograph by Bryan E. McCay.

87:   Collage by Janet Nelson Harrington. Photograph by Konstantin.

89:   Photograph by Jim Hedrich.

90–91:   Photograph by Jeff McNamara.

92–93:   Photographs by Starr Ockenga.

94–95:   Photograph by Elyse Lewin.

96:   Photograph by William P. Steele.

98:   Collage by Janet Nelson Harrington. Excerpt from "What Is Seized" from *Self-Help* by Lorrie Moore. Copyright © 1985 by M. L. Moore. Reprinted with permission of Alfred A. Knopf, Inc.

S H A R E D M O M E N T S

101:   Photograph by Monica Roberts.

102–103:   "Afternoon in September" by Frank Benson is reprinted by courtesy of Seaver Center for Western History Research, Natural History Museum of Los Angeles County.

❧❀❧

*Touched to the heart, Mrs. March could only stretch out her
arms, as if to gather children and grandchildren to herself, and
say, with face and voice full of motherly love, gratitude and
humility,— "O my girls, however long you may live, I never
can wish you greater happiness than this!"*

Louisa May Alcott
Little Women